CENSORED POEMS

Marin Sorescu

CENSORED POEMS

translated by
JOHN HARTLEY WILLIAMS
& HILDE OTTSCHOFSKI

BLOODAXE BOOKS

ISBN: 978 1 85224 195 7

First published 2001 by
Bloodaxe Books Ltd,
Eastburn,
South Park,
Hexham,
Northumberland NE46 1BS.

Supported using public funding by
ARTS COUNCIL
ENGLAND

Thanks are also due to Arts Council England
for providing a translation grant for this book.

This is a digital reprint of the 2001 Bloodaxe edition.

ACKNOWLEDGEMENTS

The poems in this book are from two collections by Marin Sorescu of poems mostly written before 1989, *Poezii alese de cenzură* (Censored Poems), published by Editura Roza Vînturilor, Bucharest, and *Traversarea* (The Crossing). The initials PC and T after each translation indicates which of these collections the poem is from. The poem 'Stairway to heaven' is from Sorescu's last collection *Puntea*, published posthumously by Editura Creuzet in 1997 (an English translation of the whole book, *The Bridge*, was published by Bloodaxe in 2004). Marin Sorescu's drawings are from all three of these books.

For Marin Sorescu's observations on poetry, I drew on Oskar Pastior's translations into German: *Der Fakir als Anfänger, Gedichte und Ansichten aus dem Rumänischen* (Edition Akzente, Carl Hanser Verlag, 1992). Some of these translations first appeared in *Poetry Wales*, and a different version of the translator's note was published in *PN Review*.

JHW

CONTENTS

CENSORING THE POET

'Poetry is the tongue under which we lodge the bitter tablet of existence.'
— MARIN SORESCU

Ten years ago people saw TV reports of Nicolae Ceauşescu and his vulpine consort (the sinister one and his odious wife, as Romanians called them) being given an improvised military trial. The room they were in looked like a school classroom, and lacking a palace balcony from which to harangue the crowd, their arrogance dwindled to petulance. We, the watchers, could guess that they were doomed. Did the Ceauşescus know that? Nicolae kept his coat on in the trial room, as if confident he would soon be leaving it. A little later we were shown their bullet-riddled corpses at the foot of a wall. Another vile, small-minded tyrant destroyed. And we asked ourselves the question: how could someone so dismally illiberal and suburbanly grandiose have managed to rule a whole nation for so long?

For most of his adult life, Marin Sorescu practised the art of poetry under a regime that tolerated his preoccupations, whilst condemning them as bourgeois frivolity. On condition writers and artists could accept the Machiavellian reasons for their own survival, and did not protest too much, they were useful token ambassadors for governments which did not subscribe to "humanistic" values. Sorescu's work was even promoted by the regime. He was a clown (they thought), and what's more he was popular. Sorescu must have understood the kind of pact with the devil he was making, but what choice did he have? He could have shut up completely (a project he certainly entertained), or he could have become openly defiant, had his books banned, and suffered long terms in prison. He chose to continue writing and to walk the difficult line between outright revolt and self-imposed censorship.

The collection here is drawn from two books: *Poezii alese de cenzură* (literally, 'poems selected by censorship'), and *Traversarea* ('the crossing'). Introducing some of them at a Berlin reading in 1990, Sorescu remarked: 'Since my very first book, I have been a client of the censor's. Irony is suspicious, and so is jokes...Everything I wrote was put under the microscope. Many poems were continually returned with the explanation "it isn't the right moment" or

11

"these verses could be interpreted". I was able to put some of them into later books. Some I didn't dare to print – on the contrary I hid them so well that even today I'm unable to find them.' The phenomenal sales of poetry in communist Eastern Europe were due precisely to that characteristic of poems which makes them interpretable (sometimes, doubtless, in ways the poets did not intend). As Sorescu commented to his Berlin audience: 'The permanent catastrophe of being delivered up to censorship has its good side. You're sure to find a pair of faithful and attentive readers.' And he concluded with typical, ironising ruefulness on the matter of the late appearance of his 'censored poems' from the publisher: 'we have won our freedom, so I mustn't complain. O censors, where are you now?'

Marin Sorescu was born in 1936 in the village of Bulzeşti and educated at Iaşi, where, in 1960, he graduated with a degree in modern languages. His first book of poems was a collection of parodies called *Alone Among the Poets* (1964) and it quickly found an audience. Of that book he commented: 'In my student days, I tried to free myself from the literary type in me, laughing as I did so. I tossed off a few parodies, pulled them out of my hat, so to speak – but pretty fiercely – sarcastic and awkward poems with which I poked fun at the lyrical confectionery then in vogue.' Ten volumes of poetry, prose and drama followed. He was a prolific and extremely fluent writer. Oskar Pastior, a German language Romanian poet now living in Berlin, describes how, during the soup course at a dinner in the Literarisches Colloqium in Berlin (1988), Sorescu produced on a paper serviette a poem for all the guests, which, by the time everyone had reached the vegetables, had been translated (by Pastior) into German. Perhaps this facility was a worry to Sorescu. He sounds as if he means it when he says: 'Just as I can't give up smoking because I don't smoke, I can't give up writing, because I've no talent. (I don't understand why so many writers consider it healthier to give up smoking rather than writing; one ought to do both).'

Or, at least he almost means it. That's the way it is with Sorescu. There's dissidence in him, but there's also coquetry. He employs the direct colloquial language of the man buttonholing you in the street, tells stories, dramatises them, throws up his arms in horror, gives you a theatrical wink. As with the man in the street, so with

12

Sorescu, chance supplies him with the plot: 'I'm a slave of chance. Now what do I mean by that? I mean a bundle of circumstances of all kinds, from the most intimate, affecting just me, to the most general, or planetary area of influence linking up with the earth's globe rolling through space. (This globe doesn't roll through space, I said to myself one morning, it rolls through my poems!) And the circumstance, for example, that you were born on a Tuesday, or on the 29th February, a leap year, and you've got toothache, or your girlfriend's wisdom tooth aches, or you've just received a really nasty letter and you're feeling bloody-minded – and all this bound up with the fact that you're writing after the Second World War not before it, and not during the Punic wars either – after all, you *could* have been – this interweaving of the inner self with the outer world creates in poetic time a kind of uncontrollable motion, independent of your will, a buzz, the hum of your individual voice, which you'll never get rid of, not now, anyway, not during the marathon course of *this* life. So you have a voice coloured by your entire subjectivity, which allows a pustule to ring your doorbell, and then – arggghhhh! – invites it in! This is what determines your style, this knot of coincidental sources. This motion, your individual hum, simply waits for you to get excited, then it swiftly composes verses, shadowing your anger, your frustration, and the moments when you jump out of your skin. All you need is the hum to go berserk and you're off. You sit down and write. *Inspiration.* A pregnant word, if ever I heard one. You become a mother of inventive activity. Your ego vanishes. Even Homer couldn't do the battle of the subjective with the objective as well as me.'

What made Sorescu jump out of his skin, as the poems in this collection attest, was patriotic fury. He had to stand by and watch as his country was slowly destroyed. Ceauşescu's hatred of the peasantry, the stock from which Sorescu himself sprang, caused villages to be bulldozed and peasant farmers uprooted. Those by-words of historical materialism – modernisation, industrialisation – were the meaningless catchwords of a political programme that was empty and sterile. There was nothing to put in the place of the bulldozed villages except the vacuum of the regime itself, corrupt, self-seeking and dismally stupid. Thus when Sorescu speaks in the voice of Vlad the Impaler, as he does in one of the poems in this collection, his voice is full of contempt and loathing:

You, you're soused in such a stupefying
idleness, I have no means to heal it.
But deep in hell a lake of pitch awaits
to drown you in its fire a millionfold.

In the English-speaking world, Vlad is mixed up with Bram Stoker's spurious legend of Dracula. Actually, Vlad – this is how Romanian schoolchildren learn to see him, anyway – was a heroic, if ferocious, ruler. Having set himself the task of ridding his country of liars, thieves and crooked merchants, he had a gold cup placed on the edge of a fountain in a forest, unchained, for thirsty travellers to drink from. No one stole the cup, and the number of impaled thieves in the market place testified to Vlad's confidence in the exemplary honesty of his subjects. A bloody example, true, and draconian certainly, but not draculian. (Those readers who do not know exactly what impaling is may care to read the opening pages of Ivo Andric's *Bridge on the Drina*, and they will find out.)

For the most part, however, the poems in this collection give us Sorescu himself, an often fantasticated self, but nevertheless him. He has something of Charlie Chaplin, the clown whose joke is to absent himself, through incompetence, feigned or otherwise (one is never quite sure, of course), from the serious proceedings of life – a joke typified by the poem 'Deviating? Not me', which recalls Brecht's line *'In mir habt ihr einen, auf den könnt ihr nicht bauen'* (In me you've got somebody on whom you cannot count). Or, again, the poem 'Mr Thinkshort'. To what extent this was a cloak of protection under the dictatorship is difficult to say. There's also a strand of deep religious feeling in his work, allied to a love of his own country. Perhaps the man transpierced by the arrow he describes in the poem of that name will remind the reader of a shaman, the one who aims to resolve some sort of a crisis situation by simply taking the suffering onto himself. Or the fakir who inures himself to pain to improve the quality of his meditation. This book is full of the symbols of the instruments of martyrdom: knives, lances, spears, arrows, nails, bullets. The passion of Christ is a constantly meditated subject. And although Sorescu can sometimes employ vicious mockery – for example at those who have connived at the suspension of the rule of law and are then horrified and shocked to find the hangman's noose round their own necks (see the poems 'Pleasant executions' and 'The report'), taken as a whole, these poems reveal not so much the sarcastic side of Sorescu as the fragile yet devout person who yearns for death and resurrection, and believes in natural retribution and hell. He has a powerful sense of identification with the natural world, with the forests, animals and birds who represent the good and the incorruptible on this tainted planet. They exert a Buddhist level of acceptance and calm on him.

The poems set the "honesty" of the natural world against the viciousness of the human one. A poem like 'On the Bull's Side' is a microcosm of this conflict in Sorescu, and is evidence, perhaps, of the difficulties he felt he had with other people (see also, for example, 'Useless Insight' or 'Knowledge'). Maybe the regime had utterly tainted civil discourse, or maybe part of it was due to what Sorescu calls his 'remoteness' or 'distance', a feeling of alienation (that clowning absence again) which also constitutes an aspect of the condition of being a poet: 'Already, the spoken word is a crossed frontier. By the act of saying something, I fail to say many other things. By the act of electing to say *this*, I leave everything else I could have said aside.' In a world whose languages are being 'blooded by technical words' the crossed frontiers of poetry, he implies, will be the last refuge of the imagination. To be a poet is, perhaps, as archaic a condition as being a shaman. Speaking of how his pen seemed to connect with that archaism which, like a miracle, still flowed through his home village, he says (a propos of the difficulty of translating a book in dialect): 'Nevertheless I would regard it as the duty of some writer or another to try, especially in view of the various phenomena that cause the internationalisation, standardisation and uniformity of a language. The Americanisation of language through blasts from the daily media will cause the dereliction of our souls. We deny ourselves the use of independent and much more powerfully expressive words – and by doing so, we rob ourselves of extremely special nerves. In the end we'll be talking with mouths whose nerves have all gone dead, and congratulating ourselves we have conquered the toothache. Then we'll notice we've also lost the magic of life.'

Artists in "socialist" Eastern Europe could enjoy the particular benevolence of the state if they delivered the "message". Poetry was supposed to mobilise, praise and incite, in a word, 'speak to the readers' hearts' although, as Sorescu commented, 'where exactly the aestheticians of the hour localised the readers' hearts was difficult to say – as this kind of poetry never connected with the normal place, under the breast.' Like all true poets, Sorescu had a twofold mission. He wanted to preserve language, and transform life. His working tool was the imagination. He had no programme, no agit-prop message. His ideology was a belief in the transforming power of words, imaginatively used, and to readers conditioned to literalism he could only mutter exasperatedly:

> This craving for transparency,
> it shreds my nerves…

Opposed always to the blatant purposes of social engineering which afflict 'official' poetry wherever such poetry appears, Sorescu's poems hold up to our gaze a world in which human affairs seem perpetually doomed to descend to the level of a tragic buffoonery. The poet who writes them is a volatile character, despairing one minute, celebrating the next – his mood-swings are alarming. He can be devastatingly direct, and then chop-logically complicated and obscure. Sorescu himself remarked: 'When I no longer know who I am, I re-read my poems to find out.'

After the "revolution", Sorescu disappointed many of his admirers by allowing himself to be made Minister of Culture (from 1993 to 1995) in the government of Ion Iliescu. It's hard to say what his motives were. The opportunity to become a laureate of some kind, to become an official spokeman of the poetry party, can sometimes prove irresistible, and it wouldn't be fair to say that only true poets resist such invitations. Perhaps, also, Sorescu felt he could be a poetical politician, the kind of far-fetched ambition, one feels, that only a Sorescu could entertain. After a long illness, during which he wrote a sequence collected in *The Bridge* (forthcoming from Bloodaxe), he died prematurely on 8 December 1996, at the age of 60, in a Bucharest clinic

JHW

CENSORED POEMS

Stampă

La carne este-nchis și, spre știință,
Stă scris de măcelar : „Sînt la ședință“.
Iar la ședință spune : „Nu am carne“.
Și altul scrie asta, să îl toarne.

Pe spate-i scrie, plin de umilință:
„Nu are carne, spune la ședintă“.
Povestea, în mai rău să o întoarne,
La făr-de-carne pune dracul coarne.

Că-n piață nu-i nimic, e numai piața,
Cu șobolanii și cu precupeața,
Ce dă cu mătura și-i tot gonește

Și-i intărîtă c-un schelet de pește,
Din Marea Moartă, cică, tras cu ața.
Și dandanaua asta-n București e.

Impressions

The butcher's shop is closed. A sign
proclaims: *Gone to the Meeting.*
'I've no meat,' the butcher tells the meeting.
Someone writes this down, to shop him.

Our informer, eager to improve the tale,
minces into the meatlessness several
cloven hooves, forked tails, and horns.
A modest dish, he thinks, and smirks.

There's nothing at the market but the market.
A pack of rats and a fishwife, who whacks
a broom at them and drives them off with shrieks –

or tries to trap them with a fishy skeleton,
raised from the Dead Sea, they say, by a thread.
Welcome to the witches' brew of Bucharest.

Stampă [PC]

The big what

Even the hospital's a fridge.
This morning they found ice
in the sick men's stools.
What kind of illness is that?

In the bed of those with fever,
they put a colder patient
to avoid wasting heat.
One in ten still makes it.

Doing brain surgery by candlelight –
his own candle – the doctor
finds a question stuck there like a nail
in the cardboard-coloured matter:

'What the bloodsucking hell?'

Marea întrebare [T]

Ill-fated

I drew the Romanian ticket, Lord.
They put you in jail. They say:
invent your own crime and pay
for it by eating hay.

By giving you a cell, they save
one flat, one set of silverware,
one bookcase and an easy chair,
one poet wasting paper on despair.

My books are piled high,
carted off, and pulverised.
It's fields not brains they'll fertilise.

Our destiny is bound with lies –
bad luck to which we're synchronised
like a crane to the shrieks of its flight.

Năpasta [PC]

Peasants

At home, the peasants eat grains,
boiled over embers to make a gruel.
The hamsters, also – poor things –
have hardly a grain in their gizzard.

Peasants returning, starved, from fields
are made to turn out their pockets.
A wasteful lot. They persist
in the shameful practice of eating.

This class, as such, remains a source
of irritation to treasury and state.
A wilful refusal to breed, it seems,
has sent their species into decline.

They own the country, but simply won't
admit it. They just weep and die.

Ţăranii [PC]

The witches

Good to know the witches have been caught,
bound into a stook, beaten, tortured,
glued to the tails of their own broomsticks
and fired off like rockets.

(They knew how to tempt us all right,
sifting chaos through broken sieves,
their hot mouths bubbling secrets,
snake familiars round their waists.)

Fat years should follow this, except
it turns out the seven fat cows got eaten
by seven thin ones. Thank you, parable.

Here we are taking great leaps forward
on the spot. We think wings will loft us
to the future. We should be so silly.

Ah, vrăjitoarele... [PC]

Deviating? Not me...

No more lining the route.
No more waving my little pennant.
No more paying my respects.
No more anniversaries, the ten since then, the twenty to plenty, the
nine, eight, seven, six months since the
moment which failed to awake my enthusiasm...

As for that famous *until*...
I've lost count of the countdown.
I rise with the sun, go to bed when it's dark,
there are no *great leaps forward* for me.
If *exports are boosted to record levels* –
you won't hear me cheering, my lips are glued.
I'm not a committed individual, no species of New Man.
I don't take a daily bath in *the spirit of the common will*,
I don't *address my appointed task with relish*.
I know where we are, without it being shouted at me.
I know where we're headed, and how fast.
I know about the sacrifices, the *collective objective*.
One aim, one thought, one will...?
It seems too little for a single life.
How shall I voice *complete satisfaction*, express *profoundest gratitude*?
How can I stop you worrying?
Aren't I a model of unswerving apathy?
Look! I cannot be deflected, I'm an example to us all.
Don't count on me!

You've set the targets too high.
I'm small, forgotten, ignored.
What am I to you?
I'm only the people of Romania,
Don't count on me!

Eu, neabătutul [PC]

24

The ceremony

I

The ceremony was very sad.
They were playing gas-chamber music.
Signing our funeral handkerchiefs, we placed them
in the national archives. A consolation.

After great and protracted suffering,
faith in the future had died. In an anguish
of remorse, people shook their heads,
and suspected each other of murder.

Actually, they'd never seen the face
of hope themselves. Till that morning,
they'd never been so close. Now they saw its
flower-spattered coffin trundle by.

II

Then all of a sudden it was carnival time.
The gassing-music stopped and new hope
leapt up and roundly declared
everyone should continue to be happy.

Loudspeakers boomed with confident predictions.
Joy transfigured the assembled crowd.
And I understood, that very morning,
what ringing the changes meant.

Ceremonia [PC]

25

Again and again

Every time I eat an apple,
I feel remorse
and say to myself:

'Munched the Apple of Knowledge again, have you,
like a bumpkin?

You brainless bumpkin!

Now you'll be reading up
the pamphlets,
boning up on God's
latest policy swerves,
taking notes,
bringing yourself up to date,
again and again
after each apple:

You imbecilic clod!'

Iarăşi şi iarăşi [T]

I am the child

At the march, I am the child
with an empty stomach, on
someone's shoulders, carried high.
To be a symbol was my destiny.

That's not my father carrying me.
Watch his calculated smile,
showing off his precious son,
borrowed from the orphanage.

Pictures taken, he'll be gone.
Abandoned, I'll return on foot, alone.
My likeness will remain behind,

smiling at a future, fogged.
His weight is on my neck already,
a dazed child, as much a liar as me.

Eu sunt copilul... [T]

27

Wrong notes

Someone had buttered their bowstrings,
surreptitiously, with a suppository.
The string section shrieked off-key.
The conductor had a heart attack.
They auctioned off his baton.

– Clean up your bows, cellists!
– We do! We do! With soap and hot water!
– Rub the strings with resin!
– We do! With finest fiddle grease!
But when the concert starts: squaaaak!

– That's really queered the pitch.
  The symphony's a scratch!
  Use beeswax, moth-spunk, anything!
  The cops are breaking down the door!
  Orchestra –

  gimme an 'A'!

Un „la" de sus [PC]

Regarding the problem

Regarding the problem,
everything is crystal clear:
there isn't one.
The problem was resolved
before it was considered.
It never had time to become one.

Regarding the problem,
don't let it bother you.
In the middle of the Ministry
we've placed a pail of water
to dissolve it. All our problems
are completely soluble.

Regarding the problem,
come and see us again!
What did you say you'd come for?
– Regarding the problem.
– Ah, regarding the problem.
Didn't you get the message?
Everything's been taken care of.
There are none.

În legătură cu problema [T]

Population explosion

Cheer up, somebody's just died.
One less munching mouth to stuff.
One more pension less to pay.
Time per head's increasing all around.

Hoist the obituary flag!

Explozie demografică [PC]

Prophecies

A blind man saw the future
which was a one-eyed man
looking at the future
which was a deaf-mute, dead drunk,

who predicted
a stammerer next
saying
'f..f..f..f..f..f..f..f..f..f..f..f..f..'

forever

Proorociri [PC]

31

Quote, unquote

Every time I put the final bracket
round a quote, inwardly I feel
the secret jubilation of a jailer
banging up some swine for life,
and throwing away the key.

Got you now, you bastard!

Am închis citatul [T]

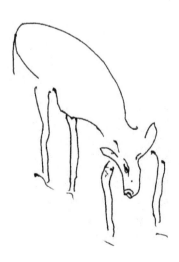

Festus interruptus

We'd eaten seven fancy courses,
we were very nearly sated,
when someone bellowed: 'Stop the feast!'
and everywhere the gourmandising stopped.

– A cup of coffee to help me burp?
a thin feaster dared to enquire.
– No coffee! Get back where you belong!
The funeral repast in hell was over.

We scrambled back into the cauldrons.
The bubbles of pitch plopped with dignified sighs.
To hell with these infernal banquets,
all the fat sins are still up there.

Pomană [PC]

Ergo sum

Talking far too loudly in my sleep,
I mutter stuff about the latest news.
I should try to keep the lid upon my id.
It babbles out the weirdest dreams.

Rebel brushstrokes place a ladybird
upon a flower in my painting.
Can a picture really be so sensitive?
Why should this retouching hurt me?

Not even Turks, who levied
tax on smoke and windows,
demanded tribute from our reveries...

...bringing narcissi, my night has come,
selling me dearly to barbarians, because
I dreamed my thoughts again...*ergo sum.*

...ergo sum [PC]

O Gods!

In the dead of night,
the wooden horse of Troy ominously creaks
at the centre of the citadel
like old furniture,
and the Trojans ask themselves,
stricken with terror:

What new misfortune
awaits us?
When the Trojan horse's wardrobe
at the centre of the citadel
creaks for no reason,
like a bomb left over from the war,
it's a bad sign.

O, Gods!

O, zei! [PC]

A new kind of sacrifice

At the side of the road,
a dog is panting to cross.
How do I explain
that the God of Roads
is greedy for new victims?

We used to offer up
virgins, lambs, bulls.
Now we let dogs breed –
incurable road crossers.

The bone is always on the other side.
But as he doesn't know the traffic rules,
the dog himself becomes the bone.

I look into his eyes
and see myself
fearing this might be
the last crossing.

Noi jertfe [T]

We live

We live as in paradise, naked.
We sing with one voice. We eat what's put
before us. God still doesn't like it.
He makes us kneel down. Makes us stand up.

Eve, with a serpent in her lap,
is showing it a trick or two.
Sin is what redeems you.
Fear can only kill you once.

So where's that famous place
where sinners shriek in boiling pitch?
At least they all owned property.
Ate chocolate.

The clock bongs hourly
A voice remarks: *I am God.*

Trăim [T]

The bones

Their bones
climb by themselves to the surface
from a depth of two metres.
Yellow and waxy.
Honeycombed.
Fragrant.

That's how you'll know them:
by the three qualities
of their bones:

The saints...
For centuries, that's how we've recognised them,
climbing to the surface,
honeycombed-waxen bones,
embalming the air.

Stop staring.
Grab a crowbar.
Whack down their skulls.
Pile-drive them into the ground.
Bulldoze back and forth across them.
Concrete the cemetery over.
Follow instructions.

No matter what you do,
from under those sledgehammer blows,
from under the hardened mud of bulldozer tracks,
through concrete, even...
they just keep climbing up to the surface,
the saints...

Just to forgive us? To bless us?
Is this the only reason
they keep coming back?

Oasele [T]

The expansion of the universe

– Peter, clucks God,
   d'you ever repeat yourself?
   My problem is, I've hatched the world
   a billion times already.
   Then I forget what I've done.
   Morning comes, I wake and think:
   what's on my scratchpad for today?
   O yes! An egg they'll remember me by!
   Hmm. But what could it be like? An egg's
   an egg. And so I lay the earth again,
   like this and like this and like this.

– Ah, says Peter
   I've heard about parallel worlds,
   with date stamps on each, and little red flags.
   I just didn't think they were planned.

– Planned? What are you talking about?
   It's the same world over and over
   simply because I forgot.

   Get the memory granules! Lace my feed!

Expansiunea universului [T]

39

A tear from the source

From the well, a single tear is drawn.
From the pail, our jugs of clay are filled.
With cupped hands, we drink the grief of elders
from an ancient, buried spring.

House doors fly off hinges.
Lambs are crushed by falling mountains.
They, and the grazing herds upon them, are drowned.
The sea covers snow-capped peaks.

Customs and good habits fracture and break.
Gardens and courtyards are ploughed up.
Why do we ask if the wheat crop has failed?

From this vortex of untold, bitter hatreds,
from far below the earth, a tear wells slowly up.
Eyes feel it coming and run mad.

Se pregăteşte-o lacrimă-n fîntîni... [PC]

I don't know how

Strange things were afoot. I don't know
how things got so misplaced in time,
how chimneys all stopped smoking, or
how it just got normal to be ill.

Slaps and rebukes resounded in the street.
Quarrellers scolded loudly everywhere.
Everyone dreamt of a memorial service in which
they'd drop each other in the collection plate – *clink!*

Even the optimists were sad.
They were looking for their own identities
with sniffer dogs. The prison for ironists
was bursting at the seams.

Nu ştiu cum [T]

House under surveillance

They've come to take my manuscripts away
with a crane as tall as a tree.
I open the doors of the pages, set free
my poems. They soar into the sky.

Lead pellets fired through telescopes
wound the rhythms of those beating wings.
My stanzas fall. With twisted grins
the hunters fire again. The words are killed.

Greasy palm upon his gun butt,
the guard is watching you, my heart.
You could be silenced with a single shot

and this house they've set on fire
is the dream to which you cling.
Become a poem only if you must.

Casă sub observaţie [PC]

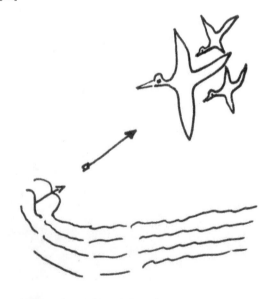

Here

I'm here, I'm nowhere.
The house itself is persecuted
into building walls of silence
which it must stand behind, locked in.

Locked inside myself, I haven't given up.
Give me gibberish, babble, double talk –
let equivocation be sweet on my tongue!
Then a raven croaks: *Nevermore!*

The gleam vanishes off the world.
This blind, ravening century has put
its mark upon the very bread we eat.

Anything I say will be interpreted
by thugs. The cop on guard outside
is trying to get my spaniel to confess.

Aici [PC]

They

They're coming. They're waiting round the corner.
Are they going to turn you in?
You're terrified. You're only flesh.
They've long claws. Bullets of iron.

Your senses cry like bugles.
You witness the murder of the sky.
They have hooves and horns.
A gun. A loaded gun.

Astride apocalyptic horses,
they celebrate their wedding with a ring
made from the earth's ellipse –

it's like the circling dance
of stars in dying eyes
and two thousand years of eclipse.

Ei [PC]

The gall principle

The principle of bitterness, the gall principle
saves us from a too-sweet Paradise.
The atom bomb that could destroy us
is the final straw we clutch at.

At dusk, you think 'I'm guiltless!'
Angelic innocence, you say, is all you need.
Your sin, I fear, is too original. The principle
of resurrection won't apply to you.

From principles to principles, old ones,
new ones, mixed together, you drink
the bitterness of life in jugfuls.

Your skin is flayed by frost and rains and sun.
Even now you cherish crazy hopes,
inventing wings from day to day. That's you.

Principiul fierii [T]

Movement

It's raining straight at the root.
It's coming from infinity.
And you, a mere ball of clay,
are goaded and pricked by buds.

Pinpointed on a map,
the atom makes a fine target.
Its flowering's a bomb,
turning rain to light.

Thin as a thread, your dream hangs
upon a dialectical crux.
You're not what nature's

chalked upon your face, for
death is life, life is death,
and both are a delirium.

Mişcare [PC]

The reward

Forces of nature, we greet you!
Unchain yourselves!
Hurricanes – have a hero's welcome!
A really big hand all round!

When earthquakes shatter houses
and rivers burst their banks,
we watch ecstatically –
our freedom fight made real!

Catastrophe is what we want.
Calamity's our lifeblood.
To prove how fearless we are,
we wage a war on ourselves.

Smiling and destroyed,
we go up to claim the bone...

Folosul [T]

The arrow

Wounded, he'd have
been lost in the forest,
had he not followed the arrow.

More than half
of it
protruded from his chest
and showed him the way.

The arrow
had struck him in the back
and pierced his body.
Its bloodied tip
was a signpost.

What a blessing
to have it point
a path
between the trees!

Now he knew
he'd never again
go wrong

and he
wasn't far
from the mark.

Săgeata [T]

Two nightmares

Two nightmares were strangling each other.
Trapped between them, whiter than a sheet,
I tossed and turned, with no way out. Each
of them slipped nooses round my neck.

Bravo! Bravo! I had to cheer the way
they used me for a dummy drop.
I kept applauding, ran the gauntlet of
their beatings – hangings, rather – till

exhausted dawn broke through me.
Daylight brought the lynching mob, reality,
wolfhounds snapping at my heels.
Again and again they caught me.

Bravo! Bravo! I kept on clapping as they
strung me up, made sausage meat of me.
How glad I was when all, at last, went quiet,
and they carried off my head upon a plate.

Două coșmaruri [PC]

49

The duel

(to Grigore Vieru)

Let's choose forbidden thoughts as weapons.
You state a fact, I'll groan a curse.
When you see the doors left open,
you'll clap your hand to your mouth.

Let neighbours crowd into the yard.
Let them take down everything we say.
Let's have witnesses, with gloves and badges.
Let's sign on the line and get a receipt.

Let it be like a firework display.
Let it be a carnival of the spirit.
Let's expose the collaborators.
The world knows what we say is true.

Caustic words alone just get you killed –
better die a fighter in a duel.

Duelul [PC]

Pretext

On the simplest of pretexts
grief enters your house,
rifles your shelves and drawers,
till you rise from your meal, weeping.

It turns you inside out and lets you go.
'Sorry, old boy...must be an error...'
On the left side of your chest
a huge tear weighs you down.

Life goes back to normal,
although you're weaker, paler.
You crack a joke and try to exist.

Porter of your own fate,
you put on blinkers and scarcely move
along your journey to tomorrow.

Şi sub un pretext [PC]

Landscape

It doesn't look good: it's three times harder
to put one foot in front of the other.
I think I must be in Weeping Valley.
Am I the only traveller left?

A kind of desperation overtakes me.
I want to shout, but I've no vocal chords.
Is it my turn to be a scarecrow?
Must I occupy this cursed place forever?

At the crossroads, I greet the whitened skulls
grinning absent-mindedly in a lime landscape.
A raven would add a spot of colour
and brighten up the pallor of these skies.

I'll saddle fear, ride it like a horse, and
spur it down the long road of escape.

Peisaj [PC]

The forest

Solemn and active silence.
Millions of leaves.
Millions of hands of fir tree fingers,
trembling on a huge dial.

The wood – an aspiration of earth
and stone. Fir trees, maples, elms, oaks,
so many essences of divinity.

Around me, the forest builds rings
in the trunks of the trees.
A woodpecker hammers in the nails.

It's a silence charged
with a fever of erected masts.
Where to, Lord? Where to?

Pădurea [T]

53

To play the bow

Clearly,
I'm not cut out to be a hunter.
No killer instinct.
I leave cheerfully for the hunt,
tightening the strings of my bow.
Then, stupidly, I notice it's a harp
and start to play it.

I can't hold back the music in my soul.
I let my fingers go.
The strings yearn to be plucked
and who am I to say no?

Wild creatures prick up their ears.
In subdued flocks, they trot behind me.
The bow hums and murmurs.
Behind me, I leave a delicious arc
of harmony in nature.

A cânta dintr-un arc [T]

Miracle

At the very
moment of his fall
the grass sussed it, grew
in milliseconds to a tall
soft wave.

Gravity was
defeated
by the miracle
of growth.

So earth produces
antibodies
against the damage
of its own attraction.
And grass is first aid
to the desperate who throw themselves
from – look! – up there!

Minune [T]

Gymnast falling

An acrobat up in the mountains,
captivated by the sheer height,
gapes into the abyss below
and falls.

Now, he says to himself,
the time has come to demonstrate
the most spectacular figures I know.
A double somersault with a twist to the right.
Perfect.
Two corkscrews with a flick to the left.
Again, excellent.
Three cartwheels with a triple twist...
half a quadruple Nelson...a threequarter Villeneuve...
fifteen springhanded backflips, double-screwed,
a triple unscrew to round them all off...
Astonishing!

Such success makes him imbecile-happy.
What a colossal caracole!
There are no mattresses down there, no net,
he's vaulting on groundless ground.
Careless of fractures, he twirls and spins,
performing feats made possible
by total disappearance of the ground.

The ultimate figure beckons, that awe-inspiring leap –
the goal of every aerialist – the dreaded figure 15.
It works! He's almost too successful!
Rapture! He's in a state of bliss!

'Train all you like, if you're going to fall, you'll fall.'
Far off, he hears his fellow alpinists' obtuse remarks.

Gimnast căzând [T]   Raportul [PC] ➤

56

The report

The inquisitor is writing his report:
Admittedly, there were shortcomings.
Only the corpse is to be blamed for that.
He (the inquisitor) should have worked more
conscientiously. Harder, let's say.
He (the inquisitor) maintains the problem
is one of incoherent babbling.
When the subject receives the sentence,
the inquisitor, unfortunately, (he, that is)
has to fold his arms and listen to
a rhythmically accelerated suffocation.
Naturally, the condemned have no idea
of what they're saying. The logic
of an execution cannot be refuted, but
the shortly-to-be-dead don't know this.
Confronted by the fact
of an immediate cessation of themselves,
(but only if they get a chance to speak)
they start a drivelling lamentation.
They have no shame.

At least they bring their own soap and rope.
They think it's a bad joke to start with:
'Save for the bullet? Are you serious?'
Ha ha ha! Ha ha ha!
What, actually, does the firm *do*?
Finally, they're convinced that everything
is very logical, although
one might, in places, polish up procedures.
The execution of the executions happens right on time,
but he (the inquisitor) vows to step up output.
Client stupefaction is the object here.
Over a spot on the wall, he's pinned it up:
Our customers are serviced dead-to-rights.

Everything drops smoothly into place.

Something like that, anyway

I caught the last plane, standing room only.
A bargain flight, naturally.
I saw tiny people scurrying about
like iron filings driven by a magnet.
'It's a pedestrian contest,' they said, 'like yesterday.
On the zebra crossing only. Who crosses first
will no longer have to wait.
There'll be nothing more to wait for. You see?'

When the plane was high
as its altitude licence permitted that day,
I was suddenly scared,
standing there like that, swaying on my feet, staring at the clouds.
'Stop!' I shouted, 'stop, I want to get off!
I'm feeling seasick. It's allowed, isn't it –
to feel seasick on a plane?'

And the plane actually stopped. The hatch clunked open
and I got off.
The next bit was confusing.
I didn't hit the ground, because
I'd never trained for parachuting onto targets.
It was hard from that height anyway.
So I landed on the moon.
And the moon was in her ninth month.
Gravid as can be.

She went into labour
as soon as I started kicking, squalling,
and asking to get off
– my obsession, I'm afraid –
and then gave birth to me.
An easy delivery, they said.
A second or third time, what does it matter?
(I felt like Lazarus)

58

And whether it's this planet, or that one,
it makes no difference, does it?
But now I don't recognise myself.
I keep pinching myself.
I consult wise old women,
study the zodiac, read the stars.
I haven't a clue who I am.
And someone inside me keeps shouting,
whimpering, yowling, choking on his nappy:

Stop! Stop! I want to get off!

Sau cam aşa ceva [PC]

The scream

For some time he'd noticed
the road cambering unduly
underneath him.

It was like walking on a giant breast,
billowing, swelling,
slithering him repeatedly
back to the beginning.

Pleasing? In a way.
First a lubricious helter skelter,
then up again, that kiddy crawl
towards the nipple.

The sky came lower and lower.
The stars lined up each side of him
in place of trees.
He himself seemed
more and more curved.

God!
he screamed at last, terrified,
give me back my cock-eyed, edgy,
angularity!

Rounded-off, I'll be
a perfect globe. I'll be earth itself,
but then
what about me...?

Ţipătul [T]

Fever

My right side's wound up tight,
my left has gone utterly dead.
The doctor says he can cure me
if I'm quiet and stay under the bed.

Every hour I pop a pill.
The first one, I'm a polished duck.
Number two, I feel so good it's awful.
Number three, I'm President of *Luck*,

a country where the rule of law
has broken down, and as for number four –
O skip it. Number five and
I'm a milkpan boiling over.

Ah, my left side is awake.
I think I've straightened somewhat.
I've a piece of cloth. I'm fit for work.
Let me polish railway tracks forever!

Febră [PC]

Sin

Lord,
when I'm at dinner
and some busy little body
tries to clear away my plate
with the half-gnawed bone
still on it,
that's the moment I get ready to bite.
My jaws click open.
I'm ready to spring, bury my teeth
in fat fingers.
I growl.

Tell me, Lord
where did I acquire
these vile table manners?
Was I a dog in a previous life?
What was the name I answered to?
Did I come when they whistled?

As to barking – I've not caught myself
doing that yet.
Though I did find myself a few times
by a hole in the fence.
I don't wag my tail, yet.
And I don't lick the hands of men.
I do not lick men's hands.

Păcat [T]

What if...?

What if we decide to make a little mistake,
we the disciplined ones, the modest ones,
our foreheads rubbing forever
at bars on windows?

Let's draw the sword from its sheath.
Let me strike, and you strike.
Let something unheard of happen.
Let me feel that I am, and you feel that you are.

With minds in manacles, shaven-headed,
we move cautiously, always on tiptoe,
not to offend some thug

while the soul, a fuse,
smoulders at one end and then
explodes for nothing.

Ce-ar fi? [PC]

Pleasant executions

None of them was guilty
but they were all executed one Sunday, round eight.
The setting sun flashed on risen blades.
Afterwards came the bang that usually follows lightning,
a do-it-yourself effort by the home firing squad,
or was it the butchers' squad? – I can't recall.

All executed, on a Sunday – I've said that,
actually, haven't I? – and just for fun.
They say the condemned had a terrific time.
Unaware of any guilt, they could afford
the luxury of a gratuitous demise.

How agreeable to enjoy a death like that –
and how fortunate executioners were found.
Upright, sober executioners, family men, with good records.
You have to give the people
what they want. Agreed?

Execuția de agrement [T]

Where, exactly?

When everything is back the way it was,
where will the barbarians fit in –
the ones who broke you on the rack,
plotted, sold you down the river?

Bleating like lambs, they'll want office,
the times alone to blame for what they did.
All you can do is groan terribly
beneath life's pain-spiked boot.

As crocuses come back in spring,
so do hangmen in their season.
The executioner removes his gloves,
holds out a too-clean hand to you.

At night, however, in his ugly dream,
if he could, he'd strangle you.

Cam unde? [PC]

A word with Polyphemus

Polyphemus, you've just one eye in the middle
of your forehead, but the rest of you
is perfect, why?

I get it. It's
to see everything clearly, at a glance,
without those doubts
a second eye can give you.

The more eyes you have, giant,
the smaller you are, that's what it is.
You stagger, get strange ideas, start having opinions,
and you need more legs,
which confuse you even more –
look at the millipedes...

With two eyes, like I have, it's a mess.
You can't put your thoughts in order.
Everything is black and white at once,
and you can't tell the sheep from the goats.
I'm talking about that particular sheep, Polyphemus,
whose throat you're about to cut.
No more generalisations!
I don't do that any more.

On the other hand, you have just one eye.
Perfection attained, it's obvious,
or damn nearly, anyway.
One thing I'm certain of,
I'd give anything to be one-eyed like you.
Ah, in the names of all the Gods,
pull my right one out!

If I closed one of my eyes,
I'd take a big step
towards the clarity of understanding.

I'd be almost like you!
And if *you* closed an eye
you'd be – my logic is faultless, you have to admit –
even greater, you'd be a god.
Follow me so far?

By closing an eye,
you'll be greater because you're one eye less.
Me, I'll be that much smaller
because, you see, the bigger *you* get,
the smaller I become.
It's a law of human nature.
What do you think this is, a game?
From the beginning
it was ordained –
one thing balances out another.
Can you still follow?

If you close your one eye
you'll leave me in pitch blackness.
See?
And since this cave is so sharp edged,
what will become of us?
We'll bash our heads against the walls,
me and these friends of mine whom you haven't as yet
gobbled up...
Polyphemus, everything hangs on your eyelid.
Don't let it drop.
You don't want to hurl us all
into the outer darkness, do you?

Don't blink, you old bastard,
or I'm done for.

Taifas cu Polifem [T]

Useless insight

And suddenly, I see them as they really are.
I stare and think: he's changed! or: he's not changed at all!
I go up to him with open arms: 'How are you?'
But he denies we've ever met, or
noncommittally polite, goes off with someone else.
My arms go down like pigeons hit by buckshot.
I pass from one to another, through the crowd.
Why, that's old so-and-so! My bosom pal with whom
I even went to... 'Don't you remember?'
But he pretends he doesn't. 'No.'
'I'm sorry, I didn't mean...you know...It's just...
How vividly they spoke, those easy ladies of the street..!'
And we bump away, separately, through the mob...

At last, a woman comes towards me, smiling,
and I open my welcoming arms to embrace mankind.
Man by man, woman by woman, it's as if
I know them all in person now. Truly I haven't lived in vain!
Except, she's smiling at someone behind me.
'What was it like in Switzerland, darling?'
'Ah, Switzerland! Such chocolate, Maria! Such cakes! And
        mountains of meat!'
She hasn't even seen me, and yet
she walked towards me, smiling...

A flood of people murmurs by.
All of them, today, every single one, was known to me.
Their biographies were carved in the wrinkles of my brow,
like epigraphs on slate,
millions of faces, deeds, words
and all for nothing. No one would admit to being
the person I knew him to be.

How exhausting this useless revelation is!
I sit down upon a rock,
my head in my hands.
And, cannoning against me, the tide of people splits in two
to join again behind my back,
an endless river of reflections
refusing to enter the mirror.

Iluminare zadarnică [PC]

Life making you sick?

Feeling bad? Here's the cure:
lift a tombstone tenderly
and slip under with God's blessing.
May the planets protect your sleep.

On this world there'll be peace
where life will now be death.
In the next, there'll be no rest.
On heaven's ladder, souls

will clamber up or down alone,
speechless underneath their camouflage.
But draw the blinds across your heart,
and go into your night with courage...

Secretly producing honey, bees
are fecundating death with resurrection.

Viaţa ne face rău [PC]

The hat

What's death
but the mysterious disappearance of things?

To start with, his hat disappears.
It was on his head, he put it on the shelf.
And now it isn't there.
Neither hat. Nor shelf.
Did he put it on the bed? That's vanished too.
Or, the doorknob? (It makes a useful hat-peg, sometimes.)
Ah, dear departed doorknob...
For want of a door, for want of a doorknob,
the surrounding emptiness grows.

Day after day, it goes on like this,
until the pattern breaks, and suddenly
the hat appears again.
And he is wearing it.

He sits down on the chair. Opens the door.
Puts his hand on the doorknob.
Things stay right where they are. On their best behaviour.
They let themselves be touched. Be tickled. They tickle him
in the armpits of his fingers. They giggle. He giggles.
The eternal hide-and-seek of matter. Life's salt.
Until he says, alarmed
– Wife, my hat! My glasses! Where did I put them?
– Don't start that again!
– I'm not starting, I'm continuing!

Let me ask you again:

What is death
if not the mysterious disappearance of things?

Căciula [T]

71

I and the other

I walk faster and faster,
something crosses my mind, I stop.
I turn around and it hits me, my halo
coming from behind, the active principle,
my astral being, the grain of truth,
in short, my so-called personality.

Like the stink of the beast
that betrays the hunted,
scented by dogs.
– That's man-smell, I say
I caught you. Where are you going?

– Nowhere.
I'm just following you
along the path.

Eu şi celălalt [T]

Knowledge

An extremely sociable
fellow he was,
and before he died
left a note he should be buried
five or six days later
to have the time
to get to know folks better.

Those who came to see him
were people of all kinds.
They stopped, looked at him a moment,
shook their heads and left.
It was very hard, they said,
to catch his eye.

Then he knew
his knowledge
was exactly what he knew before.
What you see is what you get.
Nothing more.
An endless flow of shadows,
a never-ending defilade
of countenances, masks.

Cunoaştere [T]

73

Lest I forget...

God remarks to Peter:
– Should a country slip my mind, tell me.
A country's just a mile to him,
a mile smaller than a pea.

For Him to overlook a pea is easy.
When He comes on earth-inspection, I say:
– You've left us out, Lord, not by your eternal
calendar, but all my life-time, anyway.

And Peter, left behind, idly pressing
lavender and ragwort in his Book of Hours,
cannot sense the odour of our bitterness
for his album full of dried-up flowers.

De uit vreo țară [PC]

Transylvania on my mind

Transylvania, I think of you.
I draw you in like light, all
the years of your millenial existence –
my country on a single breath.

Transylvania, at every step
a flower smiles, there is a grave.
You make the wheel complete
on which the rebel leader broke.

Transylvania, I hear a bell
upon a cross, ringing out ideals.
You're the whole country's Sunday
bringing me to church.

Ardealul, starea mea de spirit [PC]

Mal du pays

When Romanians
exile themselves,
they sit down by the railway tracks
of Europe.
Or at the station, if it's not too crowded.

They want to be closer to their country.
Able to catch the first train there,
at any time.

This gives them the feeling
they're not too far away.
They walk along the tracks.
They listen to the whistle of trains.
They're in permanent communication
with home.

In spring, especially,
when earth's magnetism
unsettles the cranes in flight,
Romanians sit sadly on their luggage
and listen to their homesick yearnings
in untranslatable seismic quivers
shuddering down a steel rail.

Dor [T]

Departing train

When an adjacent train pulls out
why do you get the feeling
it's yours?

Spring and autumn
you stare up at the sky, lost in thought.
Flocks of birds come.
Flocks of birds leave.
Why do you get the feeling it's you?

All my life I've been looking out the window,
stuck in the corner
of a bus, a train, a ship,
or jolted by a cart.
I've seen how trees race past me and away...
people, towns, continents.
Why do so many emotions overwhelm me?
Why do I get the feeling
of having known the world?

Pleacă trenul [T]

Through carbon paper

Another world, a replica in blue,
writes itself all over you, and so
across your state of waking, – or is it dreaming? –
an inky tide comes pouring through

of shipwrecks, songs and epic tales,
a duplicate made just for you.
My iris wide as I am able, I pray
my eye, flooded by this paradisal wave,

will carbon copy Eden, the one we know.
Let the Day of Judgement knock late
as possible upon the window. That's the way
you pray along your crooked path.

Perhaps the one who's typing me is finished?
The balance of the stars tips suddenly.
A full stop hurls me at the infinite.
A thousand times before, I've died like this –

Why'm I so afraid to die again?

Prin indigo [PC]

Dream

I was cutting the cord
of a newborn baby
with shiny scissors. It was a girl.
She slipped from my hands
into a bowl of water.
(A font?)
Quickly, I lifted her out.
She was crying, babbling words in English.

The dream resists interpretation.

Vis [T]

How to be a fakir

No one says you have to write, no one says you have to read. My own writing is simply an energy discharge, a short cut from mind to heart. I electrify myself continuously, in a state of fakir-like bliss. The nails penetrate my flesh, they hurt me. I'm just an apprentice-fakir, so the double edge of joy and pain becomes visible in me. But it's joy I hope to transmit.

I've written poetry for a long time, and I still don't know where it comes from. For me it's the highest thing there is, an almost scientific approach to knowledge, an apparatus of unpredictable laws. Intuition is behind it. It's more potent than any mathematical calculation. It sets the most profound and powerful human forces loose. Don't underestimate it.

A Romanian poet from the last century called one of his poetry collections *When I Have Nothing Else To Do*. I've nothing else to do myself most of the time, so I've dedicated myself to the task of cracking the mystery – The Mystery Cracker. Everybody knows the modern mystery is locked away in a safe, of course, at the extremity of the world, inside an iceberg. Forever.

So my irony must be sweet-tempered. Almost a smile. Firstly, no one should worry about liberating the mystery; it won't vanish into thin air. Secondly, poetry should have a crystalline shape – no wrapping paper, no baroque ornament. And though poetry some-times appears to lose its form, it never abandons ritual – myth is its natural environment, no matter what kind. It could be ancient myth, it could be what we're witnessing today: the slow taking shape of modern myth.

A unique gesture by the poet becomes whole and finds its echo in the unique gesture of a reader. Tongue-tied Homer wouldn't have brought a single hexameter to fruition without an audience of geniuses around him, listening, mouths wide open. We need to find those prodigies of the fertile, illiterate times again, the ones who could *read with their ears*.

How are we going to enjoy *The Iliad* or *The Odyssey* today with-out some of that old time emulation and complicity between reader and poet? And shouldn't the intimacy of writing pleasurably entwine with the intimacy of reading, whether the process involves reading aloud or not?

The gods will have to give us a hand here. A new period for the human race is gradually becoming distinct (the modern age) and we've no time to waste. Let's record it swiftly, using black magic spells – in up to date versions – and some of those forgotten songs you still can't forget. Material from the past will take on new shapes, verified by suggestion, sculpted by memory. And the poet, bowed under the weight of a tradition he commands, will continue to rearrange the world. Endlessly.

Postfață [T]

Patience

I look to see
if I've a world around me
fit for concentration.

Your craving for transparency,
shreds my nerves.
The grain of wheat in the ground
requires a certain thickness
of the utter dark.

After sowing it
with infinite care and pious ritual,
the peasant doesn't poke it daily, in the furrow,
to see if it intends
to germinate.

Patience,
and due opacity
in the realm
of a thousand and one secrets.

Răbdare [T]

82

Sick with writing

A book, once it's written,
doesn't immunise you from writing.
You fall ill with the virus
of the next book.

And on and on...
An eternal round of influenzas,
each one catching itself
from the last.

Bolnav de carte [T]

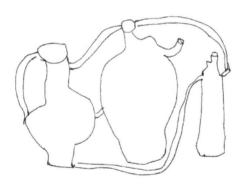

Cavafy

1

Lost at the margins of the Greek world,
like an ancient shield,
inscriptions with few
legible letters...
What they reveal are only forgotten names.
It's as if he copied his poems
from gravestones. For each one
he cut deeply
into the eye of Greek civilisation.

2

144 poems: a cemetery – for the body of an ephebe,
decaying among the forbidden pleasures of Alexandria.

3

The soul of the poet swings from a gallows
above each lapidary incision.

At the death of a three thousand year old civilisation
his poetry is a mourning flag
lowered to half mast.

Kavafis [T]

Egoism

I put fences round clouds
in the sky.
Ah, the feeling of private property!

Round the Colosseum, I put
an imaginary fence,
round the monument to Augustus,
round the whole of Rome...
I'm a soft, contemplative Odoacer...
I master all of them
for just a single instant,
happily sighing
like the smoke of cigarettes
breathed in...

...as I too am mastered
by a celestial rhythm,
and breathed in by an egotistical wave.

Egoism [T]

85

Punishment

The Dacians on Trajan's column
must pay
a daily parking fee.

One more punishment
to add to the chains that bind them there.

In their place,
for each one of them,
time after time,
I take the journey home.

Pedeapsă [T]

Fighting on two fronts

A child comes and tells me:
– Daddy, Troy has fallen.
– Go and tell your mother.
Back he comes:
– Daddy, Tyre has fallen.
– Go and tell your mother.
A little later:
– Daddy, Nineveh has fallen, too…
– Has it?
– Yes. Nineveh and Susa and Babylon…
– Well, have you told her?
– No.
– Go and tell her. Quickly!
The child comes back, a history book in hand.
– Daddy, Rome has been founded.
– Go and tell her…And since you're going there anyway,
   tell her Carthage has fallen…oh, yes,
   and tell her Byzantium has fallen, too.
The child comes back alarmed:
– Daddy, mummy has fallen!
– Fallen? Where ?
– Into the lions' den.
– Well, tell her to wait.

Since then, I've been training for a lion fight…
I have to free my wife from the den,
so we can found the beautiful city of Troy together.
After that, the beautiful city of Tyre…
And the beautiful city of Nineveh, and proud Babylon,
and Susa
              and Carthage
                    and Rome
                          and Byzantium…

Luptătorul pe două fronturi [PC]

87

Mr Thinkshort

I

Long discipline it took,
till finally he could concentrate
upon the spot, at any time.

He'd fold his arms across his chest,
or adopt the lotus,
or simply nip his earlobe
very hard.

The world around him would vanish in a flash.
A light would descend,
a living telescope
that brought the cosmos wholly into view.
(First he'd capture the earth's globe
and the solar system,
then our galaxy,
and last of all the whole universe,
the fact it really does expand
thereby confirmed.)

In the first three seconds
the daily grind would float away,
on undulating waves of the Big Bang,
dissolved as petrol
swallows fat:

Psssttttt!

The plippety-plap of himself
falling into himself, he took for the primal plop.

II

Getting back to the floating line of life
(the splashing of the dull quotidian)
was laborious to say the least.
He hired friends to slap him,
throw stones at him, call him a donkey.
They called the fire brigade
to put his trance out with a hose...
Or they stuck him in a bunker
(where even fifty metres down, he proved
he still could concentrate like mad,
walled-up, cemented-in,
to say nothing of the express freight train
they sent rumbling overhead).
Then they blew the whole thing up with dynamite,
raised him to the skies,
a height about 150-200 metres
above the clover...

...he'd wake up falling in the very principle itself,
rubbing rings away that swelled to bumps around his eyes
as big as wooden Easter eggs.

III

He never told a soul
of the research results obtained
by this colossal falling
rapturously down inside himself.
Plugged into the cosmos, he'd simply captured it!
But people (carefully lining
their digestive tracts) wouldn't have understood,
or, if they had, would just
have seized upon
the dangerous parts of his
discoveries – the usual, in other words.

89

He let slip, once,
he could never think a thought
right through to its conclusion, and so
they named him Mr Thinkshort
(to distinguish him from those
who do. The idiots.)

Sometimes
when they found him stiff and rigid in the street,
the karate types who multiplied like mushrooms
and practised regularly on walls
or bricks
would take him for a brick
or wall.

Now he's reached the age of forty-four,
and concentrating's lost its magic.
He'll do it if he must, upon demand,
requires a detailed application first, however,
signed and witnessed, saying you
agree with his elaborate procedures.

There he goes. Thinks he's
sneaking time off work again.
                    Actually,
we've had him by the scruff
for years.

Neapucatul [PC]

Am I always me?

Distance deep inside me is a cobra,
chasing me like venomous quicksilver.
Time beneath my skis goes faster.
A mountain rises up. Now the sea.

Sometimes I am me. Sometimes not.
If a pebble in the weird mosaic of myself
hurts, and I remove it, I end up
changing constantly from father into son.

It's a vicious kind of contest, this.
The reins and whip of all my being
hold me back and urge me on towards

the blazing hoop that bears my name in fire,
through which, as I prepare myself to jump,
I realise I do and do not wish to go.

Sunt eu mereu [T]

91

The crossing

I

Thousands of miles of desert ahead...
High up, a toothed wheel of fire
has meshed with the top of their skulls,
and down the ribs of their stooped backs.
The incandescent road
threatens to swallow them up.
They're like ladybirds
whose wings are scorched
by the blaze from a grain of sand.

II

Then it comes back to them, an illumination.
Beneath their smouldering feet, two thousand metres deep,
or maybe less,
there is a sea,
calmly undulating, quiet, refreshing,
at peace with itself, like
a lioness beside her newborn cubs.

III

For another week, this thought sustains them.
When their tongues parch and shrivel
and crack in their mouths like thistle stalks,
they talk again of that subterranean sea,
less, perhaps, than two thousand metres deep,
at certain places merely one thousand nine hundred and eighty.

They part the sea of sand
as if swimming there already,
and thus, like skeletons,
they cross the desert.

Chances are, within that deep,
there's not a single bead of water.

Traversarea [T]

92

Labyrinth

I misunderstood a yoga technique
and reached zen.
I misunderstood a zen technique
and reached tao.
I misunderstood a tao technique
and suddenly became a Jew.

I tried them all, the main faiths, one by one,
and all the sects,
perplexed,
as if thrown from wall to wall
by the monstrous tremors
of knowledge.

And now
what shall I do in this labyrinth,
stranded on the rock of my heart?

How shall I find my way home to that unhappy
brute,
astounding life?

Labirint [T]

93

Let them come

Let them come, whoever they are,
prophets, oracles, orators.
I've time to listen to them, still,
and till I die, I will.

Their gabble has no logic.
They strike terrific poses. Wail.
Truly, they amaze me, though
I'm never absolutely swept away.

Flood, fire, plague. It's
that old and inexhaustible agenda:
appalling cataclysm,
and how to mollify the angry Gods.

So here I am, listening hard,
a fully paid-up subscriber to delirium.
In the time I have, I want to hear
the whole damn cock and bull of it.

Let them come! I shout.
Give me fake mythology! Make me shiver!
I want to understand the world, give me
gurus, pharisees and liars...!

I listen to them, crucified.

Să vină [T]

Rhythm

Cohorts of the marginalised
rise up
and push the previously lucky ones
who held the centre stage
out towards the edge.

They hunker down. They whelp
and wait there, with fear-shrunken hearts,
for cohorts of the marginalised
to push to the centre again.

Ritm [T]

Taking the bull's part

Bull, my friend, you will die in twenty minutes.
You will impale no one.
At seventeen twenty, to be exact,
your horns' honest toss will hook the final lie,
the valour of your charge will be betrayed.

You enter the arena like a thunderstorm,
you sniff the yellow sand.
It smells already of blood – your blood.
The sky clouds over. The arena is a pupil that dilates.
You are beautiful and strong.
All the world is yours.
All this world of watchful accomplices.

You cannonball into the blindfolded nag
with an iron-clad belly,
and try to lift it. The armoured rider
thrusts his lance into your back, pushes it in,
pulls back and thrusts again.
And you, innocent that you are,
struggle to unhorse your weird adversary...
Twelve centimetres of steel!
Blood jets in freshets. You feel nothing.
Once or twice you send his pike vaulting through the air.
You are crazed and impervious to pain.
Another picador draws you off.

You change your mind, rage like a blizzard round the arena,
the red flower on your back. The sun comes out
and I see your eyes, still clear.
You're feeling strong?...What next?...A leap over the parapet?
The picadors scatter.
They're circling like wolves. Don't come back!
There'll be no justice in this struggle!

Two hooks of bone, standing proud, are all your armoury,
delusive weapons, nerving you to charge a scarlet chimera.
You reappear and everyone holds their breath.
Weak-legged from the jump, you're still a whirlwind.
Then your tormentors appear, armed with piercing arrows,
steel-pointed.
Very artistically, the first one plants them in your back.
It doesn't matter, you're still strong.
Just a little scratch, you think.
You paw the sand with your hooves.
Round the arena you go, dizzy from those deep-implanted darts.
Our eyes meet again.
I read bewilderment in those big, steamed-up stars:
'What kind of a game is this?'
One after another, arrows are plunged in your back,
arrows that flutter like little wings.
The winged bull comes to mind ... the Assyrian winged bull.
You try to dislodge them, one after another...bellowing and raking
        the dust.

You breathe heavily, stick out your tongue. What's going on?
The world is suffocating, isn't it?
You feel as if the arena's tightening around you...
It's becoming too small. What's this: applause?
The matador approaches, sword concealed under cape.
You stare at one another. Take care! He's been known to hypnotise
        his clients.
Each of your lunges becomes more frequent and more clumsy.
It's getting absurd. He says 'Olé!' and waves
his cape at you, which you charge, like a fool. Forgive me.
He spins on his heel and incites you to his other side.
With heavier velocity you charge again...to the right...to the left,
it's almost comical...for God's sake don't you understand?
You're getting tired. Don't make mistakes!
Standing away from his red rag, the matador holds his hidden sword
within it...He insults you...He yells at you...Ox!
Gore him on your horns...!
If only your movements weren't so symmetrical...
If through an error, you regularly killed your executioners, the
        corrida would vanish...

A barbaric custom would go to hell.
But you don't want to make any mistakes.
You, bull, are honest.
You keep to strict rules...
Just as we do, charging into the same illusions for centuries.

The matador has another, sharper sword.
You back off. He insults you again, makes faces at you.
You scrape the sand with your front hooves.
He raises the sword, stares at a point on your arched back.
You charge...
Ah, how passionately he implants the entire steel blade!
The shiny handle sticks out. It looks like a stake on the Andalusian plain.
Frantic applause goes on and on.

'Muerto!' whispers someone beside me, sweating with admiration.
He's wrong! But nevertheless you kneel down...
remain there, as if at your bull prayers, brought down by inexplicable
weakness...What are you doing? Getting up?
This is a true miracle!
You are on your feet, mighty bison, as if you didn't have in your
          tremendous body
the long blade of a sword.
It pierced your heart, remember!
Your executioner was a good craftsman.
Thousands of red tatters ... thousands of purple fragments,
you can still charge one, it doesn't matter which.
He retracts the sword, as if from a scabbard.
The matador is cheerful –
you fall again...this time you roll over...
your tongue hangs out...
You glimpse only the dagger blade that will give you
the final convulsion.

Acclamation from the whole stadium.
Delirium in the stands. Applause and applause again...can you
          hear it?
They're stamping, whistling, praising your brave executioner.
Only I am on your side and I cry.

You didn't know you'd die, do not know you have,
you, simple beast, marvellous god...
perfect animal, lunging at phantoms...
Three emaciated horses arrive,
you are tied to a shaft...
Straining, the funereal creatures drag you away...Trumpets,
      cheers, jubilation...

Your wonderful charge at the start
is mocked now through these pathetic horses,
trying to tow you from the ring as fast as they can...
Can you hear them applauding him? he who takes the bow?
Your life was a storm that has distanced itself from you...
They've forgotten you already, avidly staring down
at the rakes which are smoothing the sand, long-hailing your
      executioner.

Only me, I'm on your side. And I am troubled, crying...

[*Madrid, August 1982*]

De partea taurului [T]

How

Holy Lord, what is the magic
and infinite will
that keeps the peach in its peel,
the eye in its socket?

With things so badly tied,
how come speech holds meaning?
How is it words
don't spill into delirium?

Why doesn't dry land
simply jump into the sea?
How do you keep us, Lord, from
being eternally flabbergasted?

Cum [T]

Now and then

A shiver of the divine runs through me,
and God is me and I am God,
and we surprise each other now and then,
when our thoughts can't tell who's who.

Cînd şi cînd [PC]

Revelations

When God's got something to say,
he doesn't speak
to anyone but me.

He says Forest
and I see a a multitude of leaves,
a verdant deepening all round.

He says Water
and I see the tumbling rivers of the world
ploughing the earth
criss cross.

Then he says Man
and all at once
the fog before my gaze lifts up,
I heave myself onto my feet,
become king of my thoughts.

A sort of voltage
does this.
He illuminates the elements, life,
and wastefully galvanises everything
just for me.

In my little cloister
carved from a single tree trunk,
I sit electrified and listen to Him preach
the message of a single word.

Stunning, isn't it?

Revelaţii [T]

102

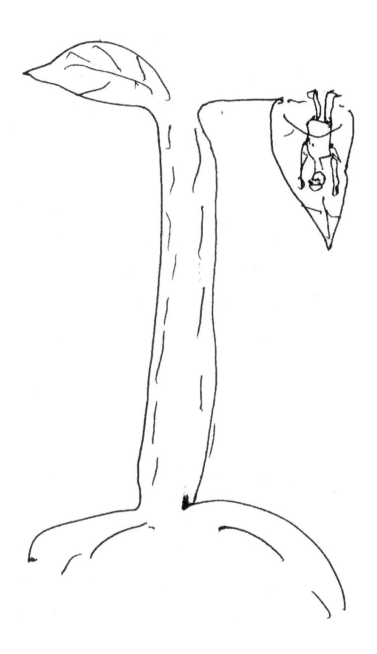

The martyrs

Just the usual lion-fodder, no one
whose name will ever make the calendar,
anonymously rattling into death.

Fed to bestial mud, your bodies are
frail as flowers. The life that you enjoy
will have to be the next one.

To carry off a crucifixion, talent
is required. It takes skill, as well, to plunge a trident
deep in someone's throat. The goggling
crowd awaits the miracle to follow,

which won't, of course, take place.
There's just an ugly pool of blood
where the ripped-to-pieces die. That's it.
Matinees on Tuesdays. Bring a friend.

Martirii [PC]

The Impaler speaks

Transpierced, in agony, you're like
manure on a fork. When a seed
is planted in the ground,
it needs a hole, driven in.

No atrocity, no apocalyptic
anguish could be like this.
I take the comet's whip, and
brand your shoulder with a lily.

My character was steeped in sloth.
Elected as your ruler, I starved myself
of sleep and rest in penance,
to show the world this princely face.

You, you're soused in such a stupefying
idleness, I have no means to heal it.
But deep in hell a lake of pitch awaits
to drown you in its fire a millionfold.

Țepeș [T]

Jesus

Pricked by lances, thorns and nails,
supported by his own pain,
he searches for a loophole in his mind

between an agonising death and resurrection.
From toe to head, his blood is rising,
trickling backwards, on old mysteries.

His powers vanished, he gave up his soul –
the crucifixion was acomplished.
Becoming one with heaven, his soul is like
a drop of water reaching the sea.

With smoothed forehead, he seems asleep,
breathed in by Heaven's kingdom.
And yet, through all the endless sleep of death,
an ingrown toenail jabs.

Isus [PC]

The resurrection of Lazarus
(variation on a theme)

If God brings me back
a second time,
I'll show you!
I'll do such things! I'll do such things!
Fury makes me speechless to say what.

You better pray He doesn't notice me,
just keeps going,
doesn't monkey round with death
because He's bored,
because a miracle is what He feels like doing.

I'm His candidate so I should know —
a brilliant choice for resurrection.
I'm the wonderful example
He needs.

Look out!
Pray hard as you can!
On your knees, implore Him:
Once I'm dead and it's official, Lord,
leave me in official peace!

Amen!

Învierea lui Lazăr (Variantă) [T]

Polyptych

I *The One on the Right*

He's a real pain-artist. A vicious crack on
my head to stop me screaming, then he wires
my ankles, hammers nails through them, yanks
my own out, mother-of-pearl, with pliers

and grunts. My men will need another leader now.
One day I'll be cast in bronze to gather pigeon shit.
The quest for truth is definitely harmful to your health.
Blackness rips me. The death tree wobbles upright.

Spat on. Jeered at. Stabbed. Ten bleeding toes.
I rode with camel-soldiers. I was their chief.
In my head, I seem to hear their voices rise in battlesong.

People mutter: That's the terrorist, the saboteur, the thief.
They break my legs and dump me for the crows
to peck my eyes out. Going, going...gone.

II *The One on the Left*

That's the ear they smashed. What d'you say?
I've never heard such miserable ravings.
Who said religious affairs would be a piece of cake?
I know we're on Golgotha! Gimme a break!

You know that's blasphemy, that stuff?
Could get you into trouble if you weren't...ha ha...
in it up to here already. Listen. I'm bleeding out
my manhood here. Spare me the crap.

It's a case of shoot the messenger, as usual.
What did I do but report your deluded spoutings?
Tell you what. Take me with you, and I'll shut my trap.

Just my little joke. Well, try some vinegar!
If you think keeping yourself alive's
a help, it's helpful. Guard! Bring vinegar!

III *A Guard*

If Caesar ever hears this resurrection tale
tryna hump some warm and whimpering slave
who can't quite make him rise to the occasion,
I wooden put it past the empra to turn nasty.

Who says we gotta change the date?
You been reading *The Golgotha News*?
A heathen? Me? Shove a spear in the son of God?
Roll the fucking dice. That was the King of the Jews!

We got more than plague and drought and leprosy.
Giraffes get taller, zebras stripier, pussy
tighter, monkeys cleverer. It's called malaria.

So tell me, what's the quickest way to heaven?
O really? Through a hole in the horizon?
Give the bastard vinegar and gall. He's raving.

IV *The One in the Middle*

Centurions with flap-eared helmets keep watch.
Leaning on the cross, their eyes turn to the woman
who weeps and weeps a little way off.
Before your tear dries, they pierce you again.

The earth is drinking drops of blood that trickle
down your naked thigh, and fall. I'm a soul
in chains, my thoughts in a thornbush of prayers.
Your unbroken, nailed image seems to call.

Thieves to the left, and thieves to the right.
They stretch as far as Rome. Justified impalements!
Pity the mother who brought them forth in pain!

Even grimmer times seem to be approaching.
Even bigger changes will take place.
Forgive them, Lord, for ever and ever. Amen.

Poliptic [PC]

111

Elegy

This zone is cursed by people and
by stars. It's marked with a cross,
which everyone carries on his back
to make a bridge betwen disasters.

Here's where the mad wind
met the vile ogre and the evil witch.
In this place, the innocent are guilty,
and pay with floods of tears.

The vanished peasant has become a myth.
As fog loiters over stamped-out hearths,
gypsies descend on ghost villages,
and old hatred rises like new bread.

St Peter used to walk round here with someone
...what's his name? They stoned him.

Elegie [PC]

Weave

Like any guardian
of the golden apples,
I'm fighting sleepiness.

Nodding off,
my chin rhythmically touches
the point of the lance.
More likely, I think,
the lance will go blunt from this chin-bounce,
than sleep be chased away completely.

What was that? Did I imagine something?
Strange wings flutter around.
I should be all ears and eyes,
but my lids fall heavily like shutters.

I know
it's the apples that give off
this sweet torpor, strange magic,
lapping the dead of night in a concentric wave,
luring dragons...

Golden apples, bewitched for sure,
ripen at the top of the tree –
a single trunk with two boughs
I've lost myself beside, forever...

Tors [T]

113

Fairytale

By the roadside,
through clover, bindweed, clinker and chemicals,
Angina Pectoris,
the last miraculous stallion
for our time
was grazing and snorting
nervously.

The saddle on its back was clammy with sweat,
and a thick vein seemed stuck in its throat,
like a gulped-down hitching post,
spasming
and struggling to get out.

With leaden eyelids,
all the brave young men were fast asleep,
hands on their hearts.

Poveste [T]

Idyll

In the meadow,
the youth was fast asleep
with his head in Death's lap.
She was grooming his hair
with great tendernesss,
and zapping his memory-banks.

She was beautiful – Death –
unspeakably so.
And he dreamed
of sleeping in a green meadow
beneath a wheel-shaped tree,
with his head in the lap of his keeper.

His head in the lap of the reaper.

Idilă [T]

115

Imponderability

OK, OK,
my body weight has vanished, I'm floating.
But the weight I used to have –
where is it?
Who took delivery of it?
Who signed the receipt?

Nobody's saying a word.
But the body weight of a man
is of great value these days, isn't it?
The body weight of a man – not in gold –
is simply worth its weight in weight.
So who took mine?

– Listen, you whining creep,
you groused when you had gravity,
now you don't, you grumble still.
Just see what weight you end up with
when you topple into the pitch.
This is just the start.

Imponderabilitate [T]

116

Stairway to heaven

A spider's thread
hangs from the ceiling
just over my bed.

Each day, I observe
its slow descent.
They've taken the trouble, I say,
to lower from above
a ladder
that reaches to the sky.

I've lost gruesome amounts of weight,
I'm the ghost of what I used to be.
Yet I think my body
will be too heavy
for these delicate rungs.

Soul, you go first.

Sssh! Sssh!

Scară la cer
[5 November 1996]

DON'T BURN THE TRANSLATION – YET

Some reflections on translating
Marin Sorescu's *Censored Poems*

An image that occurs in this book of poems, deeply impregnated with Christian symbolism as it is, is that of a human soul groping its way to an inscrutable, possibly deeply forgetful, heaven – whilst mankind plays tragic games in a corrupted garden. Did Marin Sorescu believe that his own idiosyncratic language, the language within a language in which poems are always written, would bring him closer to the 'pure language' of Heaven? Perhaps every poet, in one way or another, believes that. And what would that language be like? The original Adamic mode of address to Eve, perhaps, the language the builders of the city of Babel spoke before the Lord hastily substituted a plurality of tongues for the one: *And the Lord said, Behold, the people is one, and they have all one language; and this they begin to do: and now nothing will be restrained from them, which they have imagined to do...?* God's purpose, obviously, in foisting a multitude of languages upon the earth was to rein in humanity's collective imagination. Perhaps this patriarchal strategy was successful (there are various schools of thought on the matter). It is at any rate a situation which poets – poets in particular – try to redress.

Linguists might pragmatically suggest this notion of a pure language stems from the adult memory of that unique moment in development when the powerful capacities of childhood, as yet unweakened by habit, tradition or prejudice, could absorb the language of the environment like blotting paper. The German philosopher Walter Benjamin has suggested, in his essay *The Task of the Translator*, that the act of translation is a way of actually bringing this pure language (*die reine Sprache*) back into consciousness. In his view, the translator's function is to demonstrate the fundamental kinship of all languages. That such kinship exists seems uncontroversial. For example, the transformational grammar of a linguist such as Noam Chomsky postulates a universal or 'deep' grammar underlying all languages to which the 'surface' grammar of an existing language can be shown to relate. Thus the individual distinctiveness of, say, Chinese, Italian and Tagalog, constitute mere surface variations concealing fundamental linguistic universals. One might say that existing languages are the pieces of a broken bowl, complementary but never alike. What is unusual about Benjamin's proposition is the notion that the work of translation can be seen as an attempt to recompose those shards that languages hold in common, striving to produce hints of an original whole. At a stroke, he releases translators from the forced choices of liberty or licence by declaring the freedom to recreate, in opposition to the 'academic' ideology of translation which declares a 'faithful' translator must serve the limitless requirements of accuracy. He asserts the translator's freedom to complete his task without feeling shackled by the obvious limitations we all know about, where rhythm, metre, grammatical structure, lexical morphology, word order etc. will all be, of necessity, at almost complete variance with one another from language to language.

Benjamin was almost certainly drawing on the Jewish tradition of biblical exegesis for this idea. The holy texts of ancient Hebrew were not merely translated for the scattered Jewish peoples by its priests, they were re-written. What was practised was exegesis in the real sense of the word, an elaboration, a reconstruction of the sense, an interlinearity and interpretation of sacred writ. *Die Aufgabe der Übersetzer*, therefore, gives back to the translator the freedom of the distance that gets close. The common formulation that a translation "serves" an original, implies too abject a dependence on an original, the false promise of 'closeness' that may actually be a complete illusion. Of course all translation is, in some sense, an illusion, a sleight-of-hand – but does not licence – in the hands of a skilled workman – carry with it its own authenticating energy? And isn't fidelity too often just another bit of cultural fossilisation? The translator knows people will question his work with regard to its accuracy. He's pretty sensitive on this score. He knows very well, for instance, that the literal-minded call first for a paraphrase of an original poem as a step towards understanding it. On the other hand, the translator knows nothing is more deadly to the life of a poem than to surrender the qualities which made it a poem in the first place by rendering it as prose.

The translation of poetry is a different proposition from the translation of prose, the fundamental difference being a matter of degree of intensity and focus. Not just for the faintly abstract purposes of demonstrating the kinship of all languages (and the kinship of those who speak them), but also for demonstrating that poetry is a property in language which can be very well conveyed in another, translation is the essential work of any culture that hasn't succumbed to arrogant complacency. Robert Frost's defeatist remark that 'poetry is what gets lost in the translation' needs to be consigned to the dustbin, where it belongs. Of course, translation is always secondary to the original in its 'truthfulness': it remains an echo. In an original work, form and meaning constitute an indivisible unity, but a translation may take numerous forms, and the form's hold on meaning grows ever more tenuous in its translated version. This is why such work is a never-ending process. Translations decay and have to be replaced by others. A story by Jorge Luis Borges describes an ideal map which covers the empire down to the last detail and which is subsequently abandoned by following generations, leaving the elements to take their toll. Its ruins may still be contemplated, in a desert inhabited by beggars and animals.

As the translation crumbles, leaving the original beneath its map to gleam tantalisingly with originary light, we may very well ask, with Benjamin, why then does a translation exist? Is it merely there to enable a reader to understand something he can't read in the original? Well, yes. That too. The fundamental impulse towards the practice of translation must, however, be a groping towards confirmation of our common humanity. The opacity of a foreign language constitutes a provocation to which the translator feels obliged to respond. By doing so, he also makes a gesture of recovery towards that obscurely remembered 'pure language'. Just as our own humanity must at times seem strange to us, as indeed a poem may seem strange on first reading, we struggle to establish the truth of that strangeness by exploring back towards origin. Poetry translation exists out of a welter of needs and stimuli, different perhaps from the impulse that propels a writer towards original work, but certainly related. The poet engaged upon his own work weaves the language into a compacted form, enclosing his meaning ever more tightly so that what it holds promises, like a bud, to exfoliate in the reader's mind. The poet engaged in translation, on the other hand, tries to express in his own language what he glancingly detects in another's, endeavouring to untie the dense, unsolvable knot of language and release what is in it. Thus, in his own language, that universal, pre-Babelian language which is under the spell of another is liberated. Benjamin comments that the translator 'frees the language imprisoned in a work in a recreation of that work'.

Whispering in the machines of all the earth's languages is the ghost of an original language, to which the translator puts his attentive ear. Often he is perceived as a vandal, disturbing the temple in which a precious original is enshrined. Doors are thrown open. Windows shattered. Who is this hooligan trying to prise apart what the sanction and custom of readerly appreciation have worked to fasten together? Actually, he's really more like an estate agent than a vandal, sizing up a property, tramping through the empty rooms, noting their shape, their possibilities, preparing in his mind the description of them which will catch the would-be purchaser's attention. Can we imagine an estate agent motivated by goodwill rather than financial gain, whose object is to bring together those who would otherwise not have found each other, appraising not merely the appeal of a certain kind of architecture, but also the history of those who lived there, detecting personality and emotion in the placing of a door, the curve of a staircase, quickly and intuitively estimating a building's appeal to the present? One imagines this estate agent, perhaps, lingering in an ante room, meditating upon the seductively complex panoply of reasons that caused the building to be there in the first place.

Some people maintain that certain works are 'untranslatable' – but Walter Benjamin deflects this idea: 'The higher the level of a work, the more does it remain translatable even if its meaning is touched upon only fleetingly.' The notion that a complex work might be, in some sense, more readily open to translation than a simple one must be startling to the sceptic. Confronted with highly-wrought literary writing, however, the translator has to find expression for a residue, rather than for the words in which it is concealed. This, in itself, is a liberating factor, loosing the bonds tied by a merely functional message. For that residue, in fact, constitutes another, universally expressive language, infinitely comprehensible in a way that the inadequate communications of men are not. To translate such work is to discover a source of power. The words of a poem are placed at poles of attraction and repulsion – in contrast to the mostly static-free, discharged ambiance of prose – so that they co-exist in a state of magnetised tension with each other. The language of poems, we say, is charged – 'heightened' was the romantic term for it. Inherent weaknesses in human communication are thus revitalised and strengthened through the subversive patterning of poetry. The translator is liberated by the very nature of poetry to recover something hidden, something he may even pass on in a hidden form, without quite grasping it.

A translator is deemed to be qualified for the job – on accuracy's behalf at least – if he is deeply familiar with the foreign language he is to translate from, well-acquainted with the culture of its users, and a competent poet in his own tongue. This is why Marin Sorescu has two translators, one native speaker of Romanian, and one – I hope my readers will allow me this – poet. What we have tried assiduously to do is to domesticate the Romanian poems in English, without losing any of their original strangeness. I have taken liberties with them and Hilde Ottschofski has reproved me and brought me to heel, only to find a while later that the liberties are creeping back. But at least we know why the departures from the original are there.

We began the task of "carrying over" Sorescu into English by trying to establish a loose "crib" for each poem. This was not so much a matter of disentangling a message, as unravelling semantic polyvalence, plotting the associations and connotations of the original Romanian, tracking the spirals of metaphor, trying to locate, above all, the indefinable residue which constituted the poem's originary force. Hilde Ottschofski gave me the words, the meanings, and sometimes the only dimly-perceived intention, my role was to weave the threads. In the back of our minds was knowledge of reproaches commonly directed at translations in which the perpetrator is accused of having written his own poems on the back of another. This undercurrent of anxiety was the stream which carried us along.

Often we tried to conjure the poet himself. Marin Sorescu's sense of the village dialect he grew up with was very strong. He abhorred the 'internationalisation, standardisation and uniformity of language', its 'Americanisation through blasts from the daily media'. Like all poets struggling to purify the language of the tribe, nauseated by the lies of advertising, the blatant misrepresentations of politicians, he sought to recuperate the intimately 'special nerves' of childhood language and revitalise the enervated jargon of adulthood. What poet, after all, does not try to do that? And if somewhere inside himself he ever held a belief, however intuitively, that by writing poetry he might recapture 'the pure language' of Adam, the implicit hubris of such a belief must have made him uneasy. If God's purpose in creating Babel had been to apply restraint to humanity's collective imagination, would that not be a rather paradoxical situation for a Christian poet to try to redress?

Out of such paradoxes poems get written.

The process of mediation between the language of a translator and the language of an original poem was likened by Benjamin to the construction of a house of cards. Each card is laid carefully upon another until, finally, the last card is reached, placed on top, and the whole thing collapses. For last card, read *last line of the poem*. Why is the last line always so difficult? Presumably because, like this brief comment, it contains everything that precedes it.

JHW

The Chief Speaks

Write write! Read, read! Poetry heapbig communication energy discharge. Quick mindheart trail. Poetry medicine man go nailbed trance. Him continuous selfelectricity bliss. Ulululu! Hurtmyflesh! Learn poetry blanket smokeverse. Bigtime startnew! Read doublesided nature joypain! Read poetryearthmaker joymessage! Good vibrations!

Me long time poetry medicine man. Whiteman knowledge no true shaman guessknowledge. Whiteman firemouth iron horse knowledge. Me go tribeheart highpeak mystery hunting ground. Make good smokeverse. Send bigstrong heap powerful tribestory message. Whiteman firejourney nowhere. Poetrytribe goodplace storysmoke anywhere.

Me nothing-else-to-do man. Me poetryman. Me nothing-else-to-do poetrymysterycracker man. Go highpeak hunting ground. Crack heapbig mysterynut!

Whiteman not worry mysterygone. Whiteman not care lose mysterynut. Me find it. Make goodcloud poetrystory. Make strongbrave poetry story Make cloudspirit mysterycrack poetrystory. Heapgood vibrations. Oweee!

Oldtime poetrysmoke make reader happy. Oldtime versemusic good spellthing. Tribe listen. Tribe dance. Old time poetrymedicine man lose magicpoetryspell. Oldtime poetrymagicspell go faroffplace. Tribe no listen. Tribe no dance. Tribe go fishing. Tribe play lacrosse. Tribe drink heapbig firewater. Heapbig sadtribe falldown falldown. Need poetrymagic ear reading! Need poetrymagic listen reading! Ulululu! Oweee!

Oldtime storybook poetryman longtime dead. Newtime poetryman no good tribe mysteryspeak. Newtime poetryman need bigreaderfriend. Newtime poetryman need listenreader. Newtime poetryman heapbig difficult situation.

Earthmaker say newtime come. Earthmaker say newtime no bigfriend reader yesterdaytribestuff! Quick quick oldtime smokeverse poetryman! Make memory newshape! Ulululu! Oldtime smokeverse poetryman him bigload heavy steephill poetrywalk! Him no like walkheavy uphill. Earthmaker bigfriend oldtime poetryman. Earthmaker say poetryman make newtime quickquick. Make newtime downhill whizzfast cloud true! Make walklight uphill whizzfast skynew! Ulululu! Oweee!

Bigfriend poetryreader! How!

Postfata [T]